AF221206

j. t. baka

transvariations (explicit)

one album of lyrics

night's duty

transvision

transmission

transition

transformation

translocation

transtopia

for

you

and my utopia

galaxy cake

amélie wanted

but not available

a mermaid instead

played her part

and was killed by a dart

a blue spider

would have done better

even laureline

eating a bird alive

agrees after

consulting scarlett

letters

only in hindsight

the future tastes better

in the great wide open

of a prison cell

but at face value

the bridge is flooded

the gate is shut

and the mirror broken

shattered lies the past

aghast and that fast at last

so what

so nut

just wait for the real pain

in real rain

to slain what you can't

refrain

from

some day

it will be okay

or

alright

as the mermaid said

when they went astray

on their milky way

to be husband and wife

in a cake galaxy

transit

staring out of the window

and into the night

watching the light pouring out

of the windows of the condominiums

surrounding mine

like spaceships

they are crossing the empty void

between cold suns

looking at the fires

burning down the houses

in the center of the city

I don't know when it started

I don't know when it became a habit

staring into the mirror over the sink

confronting me with the wreckage of my
face

watching sharp lines melting

ballooning out of shape

like the mirror itself

bubbling outwards

until it pops and bursts

thanks to the heat

from my body on fire

I don't know when it started

I don't know when it became a habit

staring at the body

next to mine

watching the heat

exploring it

bit by bit

part by part

pain by pain

pain for gain

loving the open emptiness between

her spread legs

filling hers with mine

until the heat explodes

into a kaleidoscope of burning flesh and
blood

I don't know when it started

I don't know when it became a habit

but I have to stop

and I know how

staring at my meds

staring at the pills

that kill

you see

see you

soon

oblivion

flowers blossom in rain

in their mini skirts and flip-flops

at the roadside

they are waiting

what for

they don't know

maybe for their time

to come

definitely not

for the night

when they end up

in the gutter

drifting

like a future

lost and forgotten

transgression

physical examination

the doc asks

me

have you ever been

diagnosed

with past or future

at first

I don't know what

to say

but then

I want to tell him

I am here

because I applied

for the present

looking him straight in the eyes

on seconds thoughts

I just want

to diagNOSE him

I just want

to shoot him

down

for good

but in the end

it would have solved

just a problem

not the problem

fuchur fuchur

living in the past

of the future

fuchur fuchur

the future

as my childlike empress knows

fuchur fuchur

the future

will be going to be perfect

unmasked love

looking out the window

into the night

lights in the dark

houses roaming like spaceships

silent through the black void

looking out the window

into the night

lights in the dark

houses on fire

the city is burning

like an effigy

right in front of me

walking away from the window

I feel the fire shadowing me

even to the bathroom

the shadows are following me

mirroring my red hair

in the reflections of the mirror

fleeing to the bedroom

I stop in the door

the flames are already

engulfing her body

cauterizing the emptiness

I left behind

looking into ashen darkness

crumbling

I feel the cold of a dead lover's embrace

I feel me

transtopia

looking down

I see

the mountains

with their white caps

and their green valleys

with their blue lakes

and their villages

I see

a road connecting

one village with the other

walking along the road

I see

the sky above me

the white and the blue

painted on the canopy

and the gold of the sun

in its center

walking along the road

I see

the houses left and right

the front yards

with their green grass and white and yellow
flowers

and their little paths to the front doors

with their doorbells and purple flowers

next to the entrances

walking along the road

I see

the road

the cracks in the road

and the weed

and the ants in there

looking up

I see

the cracks in the road

the seeds taking root in there

the weed growing there

and the ants walking there

looking up

I see

the houses left and right

with their gardens

looking up

I see

the blue sky with its white clouds

and the sun in its center

I see

me

looking down

I see

the mountains

with their ice and snow

with their forests and lakes

with their villages and the road between them

I see me

mirroring me

I am the light

and the way

seeing home safely

the ones

I love

crepuscular

blossoms in the rain

at the roadside

in their mini skirts and flip-flops

droplets in their hair

radiating youth

impatience

they are

waiting

what for

they can't

tell you

'cause

they don't

know yet

they just know

that they are

you know

they just

have a feeling

you see

and so

they wait

maybe for

their time

to come

or maybe

just for their

deflowering

after which

dear ladies and handkerchiefs

they end up

being

tossed outside

where they will find themselves

drifting in the gutter

drifting in oblivion

like a future used

lost and

forgotten

transition

staring out of the window

and into the night

watching the light pouring out

of the windows of the condominiums

surrounding mine

like spaceships

they are crossing the empty void

between cold suns

looking at the fires

burning down the houses

in the center of the city

I don't know when it started

I don't know when it became a habit

staring into the mirror over the sink

confronting me with the wreckage of my
face

watching sharp lines melting

ballooning out of shape

like the mirror itself

bubbling outwards

until it pops and bursts

thanks to the heat

from my body on fire

I don't know when it started

I don't know when it became a habit

staring at the body

next to mine

watching the heat

exploring it

bit by bit

part by part

pain by pain

pain for gain

loving the open emptiness between

her spread legs

filling hers with mine

until the heat explodes

into a kaleidoscope of burning flesh and
blood

I don't know when it started

I don't know when it became a habit

but I have to stop

and I know how

staring at my meds

staring at the pills

that kill

you see

see you

soon

looking out of the window at dusk

looking at the lights springing up

one by one

while the sun sets and darkness

covers everything like a blanket

glowing whales are

starting to cruise the night

diving deep into the black void between the
stars

the stars are

shining bright

illuminating their systems

like the light above the mirror

in the bathroom is

illuminating my face

while I am looking right

in my bright shining eyes

burning embers deep in my skull

anticipating and eager

burning just for you

enshrined

by my red mane of hair

just one other place is full of hair

like this

burning just for you

just like the rest of my body

next to yours

is

burning just for you

I don't know when it started

I don't know when it became a habit

I don't know

how to stop

misanthropy

there will be blood

the bunny thinks

as the fox is taking her

from behind

that was easier done than thought of

the fox wants to say

after popping open the bunny

right when the wolf is taking him

from behind

the wolf wastes

neither words nor thoughts

way too busy is he

sinking his fangs deep into the throat of the fox

while ramming his dick

deep into the twitching mess of the dying bunny

live on tv

live on facebook

live on youtube

live on instagram

live on tiktok

for everyone to enjoy

for example by

sheep standing

in a sea of black blood

swinging their chainsaws

at the assembly line

in the slaughterhouse

halfing in two

truckloads of screaming pigs

in broad limelight

slicing in two

neat and clean and bloody

their former masters

working hard

working relentless

without knowing

that way too soon

it will be their turn

to be butchered

by lemmings

live on tv

live on facebook

live on youtube

live on instagram

live on tiktok

for everyone to follow

for example by

mayflies escorting dragonflies

to the showers

pushing trainload after trainload

of them

into the room

until there is no breathing

space left

after closing the doors

the mayflies

suffocate their cousins

by pesticides

through the showers

supervised by

a group of hungry spiders

just waiting for their chance to eliminate

every living witness

fighting

their mothers and fathers and their
brothers and sisters for air

clawing at each other and at the doors

the dragonflies choke to death

in an aseptic light

revealing every detail of dying in slow
motion

live on tv

live on facebook

live on youtube

live on instagram

live on tiktok

for everyone to jerk off

and to join in

Credits

*Written (analogue): Seoul (903 & 925),
07.07.2020 – 03.08.2020.*

*Written (digital): Seoul (903 & 925),
09.07.2020 – 04.08.2020.*

Titles: 04.08.2020.

First Mix: 04.08.2020.

Writer: j. t. baka.

Photographs: Simon Wagenschütz.

Impressum

Redaktionsschluss: 12.08.2020.

©2020 baka, j. t.
Herstellung und Verlag: BoD - Books on Demand,
Norderstedt.

ISBN-13: 9783751981033.